# Joy in the Midst of Life's Storms

PATRICIA TAYLOR

# Joy in the Midst of Life's Storms

## How to Turn
## Suffering into Joy

WINEPRESS **WP** PUBLISHING

WinePress Publishing (PO Box 428, Enumclaw, WA 98022) functions only as book publisher. As such, the ultimate design, content, editorial accuracy, and views expressed or implied in this work are those of the author.

Scripture references are taken from the King James Version of the Bible.

ISBN 1-57921-796-6
Library of Congress Catalog Card Number: 2005904063

My brethren, count it all joy when ye fall into divers temptations; Knowing this, that the trying of your faith worketh patience. But let patience have her perfect work, that ye may be perfect and entire, wanting nothing.

—James 1:2–4


May you grow in faith, joy, and
your walk with Jesus through this book.

# ENDORSEMENTS

Patricia Taylor certainly knows about going through times of suffering. Yet, through it all, she has learned to trust Christ to provide the strength and peace to get her through the dark days. When I look for encouragement in times of suffering, I look to someone who has experience. This book will encourage all who pass through the valley of suffering.

Pastor Eddie Blalock
First Baptist Church
Perry, Florida

Is your faith reaching the breaking point? Are you facing suffering, trials, or temptations? If the answer is "YES", Patricia Taylor's book was written just for you. God's plan is for his children to grow through suffering. He wants to turn your suffering into joy. As you read Patricia's story it will become clear how God can turn even your greatest trial into his joy.

Robert Vande Brake
Director of Education
Mayo Correctional Institution

Pat Taylor's book, *Joy in the Midst of Life's Storms* is one of the best books of its kind that I have ever read. Her life story and her growth leave the reader with a sense of hope and well being.

Polly Waller
Owner and operator
The Book Mart
Perry, Florida

# TABLE OF CONTENTS

# FOREWORD

In a conversational style, with the intimacy of a diary, Patricia Taylor relates her lifetime of walking hand in hand with Jesus. Her story is both heart-warming and heart-rending. In spite of a long string of unbearable hardships, the story conveys a joy that can only come from knowing the Lord. Physical impairments, financial adversity, emotional assaults, and consequences of bad choices could never be described as happy events. Yet within each struggle, Patricia's first response is consistently to lean on the Lord, find a way to grow, and manage to help those around her to pick themselves up and head for Jesus. Each trauma and each joy related in the book is punctuated with the reassurance of scripture verses. The verses blend into the story as easily as breathing. They belong in the story because they are so much a part of how she survived and thrived when confronting such difficult missions and pain. With great honesty and a gift for storytelling, Patricia includes no pretense of bravery or brilliance in her life or that of her husband, Troy, or her children, Glenn and Annette. Yet, as we finish the book, we know that there was indeed a great deal of courage between the lines in living each day. *Joy in the Midst of Life's Storms* is filled with precious lessons that teach us even in the darkest hours, we are never alone.

Deborah Zink
Taylor County Elementary School
Language Arts Teacher
Perry, Florida

# ACKNOWLEDGEMENTS

Thanks to my husband, Troy, and daughter, Annette, for their love, encouragement, and long patience as I sat at the computer day after day. Thanks to Mary Lou Whitfield for editing page after page with her red pencil and giving advice on English composition and endless encouragement to keep on writing. Thanks to W. C. Blue, my cousin, for advice on specific chapters and help with police department and investigative procedures. Without him, a conviction of my daughter's attacker would not have been obtained. Thanks to Sarah Harvey, my aunt, who never let the thoughts fade but pushed for the best. She introduced me to *Writer's Digest* magazine and other sources of valuable information. Thanks to the Southern Christian Writer's Conference for being a testimony that a Christian writer has a responsibility to be the best they can be and to fulfill God's calling as a writer. Thanks to friends: Eleanor Dinkins, Becky Lindsey, and daughter, Becky, and

Gertrude Brown, who believed in me, prayed for me, and encouraged me each step of the way. Thanks to Beverly Folsom who has been a wonderful "gopher" and helped in many ways. Thanks to the staff at Winepress for their many kindnesses and help.

Thanks to each one, without your help this book would not have become a reality.

# INTRODUCTION

Many of the accounts on the following pages have been shared verbally with Sunday school classes, in testimony services, or when sharing one on one God's love and His working in my life. Friends have told me that they too have shared my life experiences with others in order to encourage them in their walk of faith.

Committing scripture to memory is vital. The Word of God is the sword of the Spirit and a most important part of our armor as we do battle with Satan. Recently, the scripture, 2 Corinthians 1:3–4: "Blessed be God, even the Father of our Lord Jesus Christ, the Father of mercies, and the God of all comfort; Who comforted us in all our tribulation, that we may be able to comfort them which are in any trouble, by the comfort wherewith we ourselves are comforted of God," spoke directly to my heart, and I began to write the events of this book. Truly God has comforted me through every difficulty and tribulation in life and that is why I pray this book will be a comfort to each of you who read these pages.

Some names have been changed (noted by an *) to protect the confidentiality of the individuals.

The purpose of this book is to assist you in your daily walk with the Lord and give you boldness and courage to call upon Him quickly while He may be found. You can be a happy, joyful person as you see the heavenly Father working through your suffering.

—Patricia Taylor

## Chapter 1

# SERVICE

Now the word of the Lord came unto Jonah, saying, go to Nineveh, that great city and cry against it; for their wickedness is come up before me.

—Jonah 1:1–2

I gave notice in 1998 of my pending retirement but never turned in the retirement papers to the personnel office. I had worked for the department of health since 1975, enjoying every minute and every task. I was a loyal employee, a supervisor who got things done, and a co-worker who prayed for fellow employees and shared God's love at every opportunity. My co-workers and employer said, "Pat, we need you." We were in a building program (doubling the medical space) and hiring new staff, all of which were important to me. I was holding on to those words "We need you!" My decision to postpone my retirement had consequences.

My life was much like Jonah's. God called Jonah to go to Nineveh, but Jonah went in the opposite direction. This decision resulted in dire consequences for Jonah. He boarded a ship for Tarshish, was thrown overboard at sea, was swallowed by a great fish, spent three days and three nights in the fish's belly, and then the fish vomited Jonah upon dry land. Jonah finally agreed to go to Nineveh, grumbling and complaining—but he went.

Why was God's call to Jonah ignored? I was also ignoring God's call to a change of service. I had this little conversation with myself: "Someone else will not do the job as well, and besides, I can continue to do a good job for a long time."

A brown spider bite in June 1999, in addition to the treatment for the bite, put me to bed for six weeks. There was a trip to the emergency room and weekly trips to the doctor. I was not well and the medications were not helping. My mind kept telling my body that I needed to go to work. I returned to work and three weeks later was back in the emergency room with a heart attack. The next morning a catheterization was performed to determine the heart damage, and at the same time, about eighty miles away, my mother died.

"Be still and know that I am God" (Psalm 46:10). God was speaking to me, but I was not listening. Again, work was constantly on my mind; I was not ready to listen to the leading of the Holy Spirit. I worked at home during the recuperation period, and when I returned to the office full time, I discovered that I was too weak to work a full day. I hoped that a couple more weeks of rest and vacation time would make me feel better, but it didn't. Before the vacation time was over, I completed the retirement papers, set a date to retire, mailed the papers to the personnel office, and prepared a letter for my employer, giving a two months' notice. When asked if I would stay longer, the answer this time was, "No, the paperwork has already been filed." Although my mind was getting ready for a change, my heart still rebelled. Once I retired, my employer asked if I would be available by phone, and my reply was, "Of course." The phone rang every day for several weeks and then a couple of times a week for several months (all work related). The calls were a lifeline—I looked forward to them, they kept me going and gave me purpose. Five months passed, and there had been little change in my lifestyle. I began to dread the changes retirement was making in my life and the uncertainties ahead. I knew in my heart that God surely had a plan for me, if I was willing to let Him lead. My family was supportive and was willing for me to work things out in my own time.

I began seeking direction and praying for guidance: "Study to show thyself approved unto God, a workman that needeth not to be ashamed, rightly dividing the word of truth" (2 Timothy 2:15). "God is able to do exceedingly abundantly above all that we ask or think, according to the (Holy Spirit's) power that worketh in us" (Ephesians 3:20).

Little by little, one day at a time, my life began changing, and I am satisfied that God was in control all the time, working things out for my good and His purpose. ("We know that all things work together for good to them that love God, to them who are the called according to his purpose" [Romans 8:28].) A year later, the word *retirement* means a new life and a new purpose. And thank the Lord, I can now say, "Retirement is wonderful!"

The change of service is still unfolding as God renews my strength. He is teaching me the writing craft and that a ministry of intercessory prayer and encouragement of fellow Christians is needed in the Church today. All of which require faithfulness. Plus, I have received a bonus— my husband and daughter are teaching me how to enjoy little things and take pleasure in them. ("Her children arise up, and call her blessed; her husband also, and he praiseth her" [Proverbs 31:28].)

*Chapter* 2

# COMFORT

Blessed be God, The Father of our Lord Jesus Christ, The
Father of mercies, And the God of all comfort . . .
> —2 Corinthians 1:3

A t the age of six, I became a victim of poliomyelitis,
or polio. I was tall for my age, a tomboy—rowdy at
times, a happy child, always trying to please, and a
daddy's girl. I had thin, straight blond hair and "lily white
skin" (my grandma always said).

One cold morning in early January 1943, I jumped up
and began making up my bed, which was a daily habit. I
had a difficult time because my right leg refused to hold
me up. It was like putty—every step resulted in a fall to the
floor. After about three attempts, I began hopping on my
left leg (in order to stay off the floor) and finished making
the bed. I then hopped into the kitchen to eat breakfast. Of
course, Mama asked, "Why are you hopping?"

"I can't walk on my right leg."

"What do you mean? Let me see." After several falls, Mama called Dr. Greene (our local doctor), and he agreed to make a house call later in the day. It was not unusual for doctors to make house calls in those days, and I can remember many occasions when Dr. Greene came to our house.

We lived in the small rural town of Perry, in north Florida. The population of Taylor County was 11,591 in 1940.[1] Perry was noted for having the largest cypress mill in the world. There were large stands of virgin cypress throughout the South, and the industry was quite lucrative. My dad owned several logging trucks, a small sawmill, and a two-pump gas station with a garage attached, where he worked on his own trucks. He left home before daylight each morning and did not return until late each evening. Mama often woke my brother, Buddy, and me at night when Dad got home to spend some time with him. Dad was always very proud of us and we knew that he loved us.

Dr. Greene came later in the day, as he said he would, put a splint on my leg, and confined me to bed. He suggested bed rest and "wait and see." Several days later, I became feverish and was delirious at night. Mama put me in her bed and told me stories as long as she could stay awake. When she would fall asleep, I felt like the bed began flying. It seemed it would come up off the floor and spin around and around. I was scared, holding on to Mama, and crying, "Tell me another story, please tell me another story, and make the bed stop flying!"

The symptoms of high fevers, delirium, and the inability to stand or walk caused the local health department to quarantine our home. Dad was permitted to come and go to work. No one knew what to do or how to treat this unknown disease. It was frightening for our family and friends. Soon a young doctor, located in a logging town about six miles away, purchased an x-ray machine, and Dr. Greene made arrangements for me to have an x-ray. The young doctor had read about tiny virus particles, called *infantile paralysis*, that attack the gray matter of the brain and spinal cord. Scientists once thought that only children got it and that it always caused paralysis.[2] My illness was given the name infantile paralysis. The local chapter of the March of Dimes knew of a children's hospital in Jacksonville whose primary purpose was treating children with infantile paralysis.

My dad was a proud thirty-one-year-old and refused to accept any assistance except a referral to the hospital. Times were hard, jobs were scarce, and most young men had volunteered or been drafted into the military. Dad got a job at the shipyard in Jacksonville, found a little house, and moved his family there. The house had no electricity or running water, but it was located on the bank of a little creek. Buddy and I thought that this was a wonderful place. Mama called it "Camp Misery." Buddy was one year younger than I. He loved to fish and play in the boat. Mama enrolled him in first grade, made arrangements for him to ride the school bus, and then worried every day that he would not get back home again.

This was a strange new world where we had moved. Dad and Mama began making plans for me to be admitted to the children's hospital for surgery. The hospital was a scary place! I did not like it, right from the start. Dr. Fort and Dr. Martin, both orthopedic surgeons, agreed that the polio had left me paralyzed in the right leg, and surgery was the only alternative for me to walk again. The hospital was designed like an airplane, or so it seemed to me. Two long wings were on the main floor, one wing, or ward, for girls and one for boys, and the main entrance and offices were in between. Surgery rooms were on the second floor above the offices. A clinic and examination rooms were located in the basement. I saw Dr. Martin on my first visit to the clinic. Arrangements were made for admittance and surgery, with a payment plan for Dad of so much per week.

A lot of new homes were being built in Jacksonville during this time. A subdivision, River Hills Circle, was close to completion just a mile from the children's hospital. Dad began inquiring about one of the houses and soon was able to move his family into a nice new house with running water and electricity. It was wonderful, and Mama could walk or catch a city bus to the hospital.

The day came for me to be admitted to the hospital. Mama took me, filled out lots of papers, signed permission forms, and got me settled in. She was allowed to stay that day until the surgery was over and I awoke. Let me tell you what an awful experience that was. In preparation for surgery, the nurse scrubbed me with iodine and shaved my right side from the waist to my toes and wrapped me in a clean sheet and pinned it together. My bed was rolled into the surgery room; the lights were blinding, and everyone had on masks and green suits. That was a scary place! A rubber mask was placed over my face, and the nurse said, "Breathe deep." It was a nauseating smell. I began to cry, and the tears were running down my face and diluting the ether from the mask. The nurse sounded very angry as she said to me, "Do you want to walk again? If so, you had better be quiet and go to sleep, or the doctors will take you right back to your room and you will never walk again." I wanted to walk again, but I was afraid. I did not understand all that was taking place and no one took time to explain. The next thing I remember was being very sick—vomiting and heaving. Oh! It was terrible. Mama was by my side, holding my hand and softly saying that everything would be all right.

The next day, I was moved downstairs to the girls' ward, and I did not see Mama again for a week. There were so many girls in the ward, all in beds. Some babies, some teenagers, one girl in an iron lung, some in total body casts, and some like me, a cast on my right side from the hip to my toes. I wanted to go home. I wanted my mama.

I was in the hospital for three months. Three months to a six-year-old is an eternity. There was a routine of school classes every morning and therapy every afternoon. Boys and girls of similar ages went to school at the same time. The nurses would roll our beds to the classroom. The only thing I'm sure that I learned how to do in school was to cheat on spelling tests. I was assigned a new spelling lesson every day. (It was impossible to learn ten new words every day and do other lessons too.) The older children would help the younger children; they knew all the tricks and were always anxious to tell you how to make the teacher or nurse happy. I had attended only three or four months of first grade in public school and had not learned many of the basic fundamentals. As a result, my spelling has suffered all these years.

Each child was allowed one visitor for two hours each Sunday afternoon. Mama was always there and on time, but there were many children who had no visitors! I became possessive of Mama's time and resented her spending time with the other children. She would rock one child and read to many more at the same time.

When the time finally came that I could go home, I was walking on crutches and wearing a brace on my right leg. The neighborhood children made a big thing of walking on crutches and wanted to take a turn, so the crutches became a bond between us, and no one made fun of me.

We moved back to our hometown, and every other year during the summer, Dad and Mama took me to Hope Haven Hospital for additional corrective surgery on my right foot and leg. The year that I was sixteen years old, the doctors did surgery on my left leg and shortened it one and three-fourths inches in order to make both legs approximately the same length. That was the last polio surgery for me. (My dad's payment plan of so much per week was not paid in full until after I graduated from high school in 1954.)

God works in many different ways. Sometimes He uses physicians and surgeons; other times, scientists develop vaccine; and sometimes He intervenes with divine healing. ("Wherefore lift up the hands which hang down, and the feeble knees; And make straight paths for your feet, lest that which is lame be turned out of the way; but let it rather be healed" [Hebrews 12:12–13].)

## Sidebar to Chapter 2: Jonas Salk, CDC Funding

Polio was a contagious viral disease that crippled tens of thousands in the 1950s and killed more than a thousand persons a year.

Jonas E. Salk of the University of Pittsburgh developed the first successful polio vaccine in 1954, and one of the largest medical field trials in American history was carried on to prove the usefulness of the vaccine. About 1,830,000 school children took part in the tests.[3]

The United States Department of Health and Human Services budgeted $608,000,000 for the fiscal year 2001 for the purchase of vaccine and $391,000,000 for immunization activities in the United States. The Childhood Immunization Initiative is managed by the Center for Disease Control (CDC) in Atlanta, Georgia. CDC provides funding for vaccines and assistance for access to public health clinics and private providers. All fifty states are participating in a program called Vaccines for Children (VFC), which was started in October 1994. About ninety-five percent of American children are adequately vaccinated by kindergarten age, yet about one million children are not protected against fatal illnesses. The federal government has set a goal of full immunization for ninety percent of all children by the time they are two years old.[4]

Vaccines have eliminated many childhood diseases, polio included. But, in order for children to reap the benefits of the vaccine, they must be vaccinated.

Children should begin a regular immunization schedule at birth, as recommended, and then receive booster immunizations routinely per the Recommended Childhood Immunization Schedule[5].

**(Attachment . I, Comfort)**

**Immunization Schedule:**

# Recommended Childhood Immunization Schedule United States, January - December 2001

Vaccines[1] are listed under routinely recommended ages. [Bars] indicate range of recommended ages for immunization. Any dose not given at the recommended age should be given as a "catch-up" immunization at any subsequent visit when indicated and feasible. [Ovals] indicate vaccines to be given if previously recommended doses were missed or given earlier than the recommended minimum age.

| Age ▶ / Vaccine ▼ | Birth | 1 mo | 2 mos | 4 mos | 6 mos | 12 mos | 15 mos | 18 mos | 24 mos | 4-6 yrs | 11-12 yrs | 14-18 yrs |
|---|---|---|---|---|---|---|---|---|---|---|---|---|
| Hepatitis B[2] | Hep B #1 | Hep B #2 | | | Hep B #3 | | | | | | Hep B | |
| Diphtheria, Tetanus, Pertussis[3] | | | DTaP | DTaP | DTaP | | DTaP | | | DTaP | Td | |
| H. influenzae type b[4] | | | Hib | Hib | Hib | Hib | | | | | | |
| Inactivated Polio[5] | | | IPV | IPV | IPV | | | | | IPV | | |
| Pneumococcal Conjugate[6] | | | PCV | PCV | PCV | PCV | | | | | | |
| Measles, Mumps, Rubella[7] | | | | | | MMR | | | | MMR | MMR | |
| Varicella[8] | | | | | | Var | | | | | Var | |
| Hepatitis A[9] | | | | | | | | | Hep A — in selected areas[9] | | | |

Approved by the Advisory Committee on Immunization Practices (ACIP), the American Academy of Pediatrics (AAP), and the American Academy of Family Physicians (AAFP).

# COMFORT

1. This schedule indicates the recommended ages for routine administration of currently licensed childhood vaccines, as of 11/1/00, for children through eighteen years of age. Additional vaccines may be licensed and recommended during the year. Licensed combination vaccines may be used whenever any components of the combination are indicated and its other components are not contraindicated. Providers should consult the manufacturers' package inserts for detailed recommendations.

2. *Infants born to HBsAg-negative mothers* should receive the first dose of hepatitis B (Hep B) vaccine by age two months. The second dose should be at least one month after the first dose. The third dose should be administered at least four months after the first dose and at least two months after the second dose, but not before six months of age for infants.

   *Infants born to HBsAg-positive mothers* should receive hepatitis B vaccine and 0.5 ml hepatitis B immune globulin (HBIG) within twelve hours of birth at separate sites. The second dose is recommended at one to two months of age and the third dose at six months of age.

   *Infants born to mothers whose HBsAg status is unknown* should receive hepatitis B vaccine within twelve hours of birth. Maternal blood should be drawn at the time of delivery to determine the mother's HBsAg status; if the HBsAg test is positive, the infant should receive HBIG as soon as possible (no later than one week of age).

   *All children and adolescents* who have not been immunized against hepatitis B should begin the series during any visit. Special efforts should be made to immunize those who were born in, or whose parents were born in, areas of the world with moderate or high endemicity of hepatitis B virus infection.

3. The fourth dose of DTaP (diphtheria and tetanus toxoids and acellular pertussis vaccine) may be administered as early as twelve months of age, provided six months have elapsed since the third dose, and the child is unlikely to return, at age fifteen to eighteen months. Td (tetanus and diphtheria toxoids) is recommended at eleven to twelve years of age if at least five years have elapsed since the last dose of DTP, DTaP or DT. Subsequent routine Td boosters are recommended every ten years.

4. Three *Haemophilus influenza* type b (Hib) conjugate vaccines are licensed for infant use. If PRP-OMP (PedvaxHIB @ or ComVax@ [Merck]) is administered at two and four months of age, a dose at six months is not required. Because clinical studies in infants have demonstrated that using some combination products may induce a lower immune response to the Hib vaccine component, DTaP/Hib combination products should not be used for primary immunization in infants at two, four, or six months of age, unless FDA-approved for these ages.

5. An all-IPV schedule is recommended for routine childhood polio vaccination in the United States. All children should receive four doses of IPV at two months, four months, six to eighteen months, and four to six years of age. Oral polio vaccine (OPV) should be used only in selected circumstances. See MMWR May 19, 2000/49 [RR-5]; 1–22.)

6. The heptavalent conjugate pneumococcal vaccine (PCV) is recommended for all children two to twenty-three months of age. It also is recommended for certain children twenty-four to fifty-nine months of age. (See MMWR Oct. 6, 2000/49 [RR-9]; 1–35.)

7. The second dose of measles, mumps, and rubella (MMR) vaccine is recommended routinely at four to six years of age but may be administered during any visit, provided at least four weeks have elapsed since receipt of the first dose and that both doses are administered beginning at or after twelve months of age. Those who have not previously received the second dose should complete the schedule by the eleven-to-twelve-year-old visit.

8. Varicella (Var) vaccine is recommended at any visit on or after the first birthday for susceptible children, i.e. those who lack a reliable history of chickenpox (as judged by a health care provider) and who have not been immunized. Susceptible persons thirteen years of age or older should receive two doses, given at least four weeks apart.

9. Hepatitis A (Hep A) is shaded to indicate its recommended use in selected states and/or regions, and for certain high-risk groups; consult your local public health authority. (See MMWR Oct. 1, 1999/48 [RR-12]; 1–37.)

*For additional information about the vaccines listed above, please visit the National Immunization Program Home Page at http://www.cdc.gov/nip/ or call the National Immunization Hotline at 800-232-2522 (English) or 800-232-0233 (Spanish).*

. . . . . . . . . . . . . . . . . . . . . . . . . . . . . . .

## Chapter 3

# SALVATION AND HEALING

And he cried, saying, Jesus, thou son of David, have mercy on me. And Jesus asked him, saying, What wilt thou that I shall do unto thee? And he said, Lord, that I may receive my sight. And Jesus said unto him, receive thy sight: thy faith hath saved thee.

—Luke 18:38–42

I heard radio announcements of large tent meetings and healing services being conducted at various places. *Wouldn't it be great if the Lord would heal my feet and legs so both of them would be the same size?* I begged Mama, "Please take me to one of the healing meetings," but we never went.

On a Sunday afternoon in 1949, I asked Mama, "What does it mean 'to be saved'?"

We had been to church, came home, and Mama was cooking dinner for the family. She turned the stove off, got her Bible, sat down beside me, and began to explain the plan of salvation.

She knew that I was under conviction. Our pastor had been faithfully preaching the Word, and Mama was the best Christian I knew. She asked: "1) Do you believe Jesus is the Son of God? 2) Do you believe Jesus was born of a virgin? 3) Do you believe Jesus died on the cross for sinners? 4) Do you believe Jesus was buried and rose from the dead on the third day, and 5) do you believe Jesus is alive and in heaven with God the Father?" She also asked, "Have you committed sin? Are you a sinner?" She opened her Bible and read many scriptures as we talked.

My answer was "Yes, I believe that Jesus is the Son of God, but how could He die for *my* sins or *forgive me* of all the bad things that I had done?" ("If thou shalt *confess with thou mouth* the Lord Jesus and shalt *believe in thy heart* that God raised him from the dead, thou shalt be saved" [Romans 10:9 Italics mine]). I wanted to be saved, but this was hard to understand.

Mama called our pastor and asked if we could come early to evening church service and talk to him. "Patricia wants to be saved," she said.

We did go see the pastor, and he confirmed all that Mama had told me and said that understanding would come as I grew and studied my Bible and talked to God the Father. Right then and there, I accepted the Lord Jesus as my personal Savior and asked Him to come into my heart and forgive me of my sin and help me to live for Him. Guess what? He did! I wish I could remember the month and day of my spiritual birthday, because "real life" began that day.

It was Sunday, a warm fall day in 1949, I was thirteen years old, and Jesus was calling me to be His follower. What a wonderful day!

A few weeks later, I was baptized. That was an amazing experience. I wore a white robe, as did each one who was baptized. The pastor said that following the Lord in baptism was an outward picture of what had already taken place in my heart. Going down into the water was a symbol of the death, burial, and resurrection of the Lord Jesus. My baptism testified to the world that I had died to sin and was being buried with Him in baptism, and as I came up out of the water, I was raised to walk in newness of life. "Therefore if any man (woman) be in Christ, he is a new creature; old things are passed away; behold all things are become new" (2 Corinthians 5:17).

The Bible has taught me how to have a daily walk with the Lord Jesus and to claim His promises for my own. The Bible teaches that Jesus healed the sick, those who were crippled, and those possessed with devils. "And Jesus went about all Galilee, teaching in their synagogues, and preaching the gospel of the kingdom, and healing all manner of sickness and all manner of disease among the people . . ." (Matthew 4:23). "Verily, verily, I say unto you, He that believeth on me, the works that I do shall he do also; and greater works than these shall he do; because I go unto my Father. And whatsoever ye shall ask in my name, that will I do, that the Father may be glorified in the Son" (John 14:12–13). I believed the Bible was true, and if I asked, in faith believing, it would be done. I had never been to a healing service, nor did I know anyone who had, but I wanted to go.

Several years later, I was living in Jacksonville and attending Massey Business College. A tent meeting was held not far from where I lived. Of course I went. The tent was set up next to the Gator Bowl (football stadium), and it was the largest thing I had ever seen. Inside was a platform with lots of microphones, and there were loudspeakers everywhere, inside and outside. There must have been several thousand folding chairs on the grass inside the tent. The chairs were placed in nice even rows with aisles for people to walk between every ten or twelve chairs. The tent was full of happy, excited people, all singing and clapping their hands. When the message was over, the question was asked, "Do you need healing? Do you believe God heals? Do you want prayer for your healing?" Many people began going down for prayer. Pretty soon the aisles of the tent were so full that movement was limited. Those of us in the back of the tent stood on our chairs in order to see what was happening. It was unbelievable—healing was taking place all around me.

Right there in the chair were I stood, I prayed, "Lord, I believe. Please heal my feet and legs." I was so excited, I cannot tell you what I felt. But the next day and every day since, my left leg continues to be larger and longer than my right leg. My shoe size was then, and continues to be, size eight on the left foot and size six and one-half on the right foot. Needless to say, I was disappointed. Did I really believe that both legs were going to be the same size and length? I'm not sure; I had never tested God's Word before. What then? I learned an important principle—God heals and I must claim my healing and thank Him for it; otherwise, Satan will rob me of the healing and take away my joy.

The most amazing thing happened, and it took me awhile to realize it—God healed my legs! They take me everywhere I want to go, they never hurt, and the difference in foot and leg size is not noticeable to anyone (except me) unless I tell them about the polio and the size differences. Isn't God good—not only does He answer prayer, but He also answers it better! Better than we can ever imagine. ("Jesus said unto him, if thou canst believe, all things are possible to him that believeth" [Mark 9:23].)

*Chapter* 4

# PROVISION

But put ye on the Lord Jesus Christ, and make not provision for the flesh, to fulfill the lusts thereof.

—Romans 13:14

I had a good job as an accountant in Jacksonville, working for a CPA (certified public accountant) firm. I lived in a boarding house about ten blocks from the office where I worked and enjoyed a picturesque walk to and from work every day. The boarding house cost thirty-five dollars a week for a private room and two meals a day. The house was owned and operated by a middle-aged couple, who treated all their boarders as part of the family. The house was a large two-story and could accommodate five men and five women at any one time. Meals were served family style around a large dining table. It was in this atmosphere that I met my future husband.

Troy was six-feet tall, had blond curly hair, and wore his shirt unbuttoned, displaying a well-developed chest covered with hair. He was ten years older than I was, kind and considerate in little ways, and we enjoyed each other's company. When it rained, he began showing up where I worked to drive me home (so I would not get all wet). That was a big deal, because traffic was always heavy in downtown Jacksonville after work—but when it rained, it was incredible.

The time came that I took him to meet my parents; they were not impressed but treated him graciously. We were married September 1956 in a small ceremony in my hometown. After the wedding, we returned to Jacksonville and our jobs.

We rented a small, furnished apartment with a large bedroom and kitchen. There was a small entrance hall occupied by one chair, a small end table, and a lamp. We called it our living room but spent absolutely no time there. We decorated a small Christmas tree and set it on the end table in our living room, although we planned to go out of town for Christmas.

Troy was an electrical motor repairman who worked many overtime hours each week. He drove an older model Pontiac convertible for which he was making payments. I had a new Chevrolet that I was also making payments on. I was concerned about how to spend our paychecks prudently; therefore, we decided to sell the Pontiac.

I was taught to tithe as a child. My dad gave Buddy and me an allowance every week. We had specific chores to do in order to receive the allowance. My earliest memory was of receiving thirty-five cents a week. My thirty-five cents was used as follows: five cents for the church, twenty-five cents to attend the Saturday movie, and five cents to spend on anything I wanted. Some weeks, I bought popcorn or a candy bar. Other times, I saved my nickel for several weeks to purchase something special. Our family led austere lives; Mama even borrowed money from me to buy bread at times. I shall always be thankful for Mama and Dad's instruction and examples in Christian living.

In the early years of our marriage, I deposited the paychecks, paid the bills, and tithed both of our incomes. As the weeks passed, I learned that Troy owed many bills, to several loan companies, as well as some of his friends. It was a juggling act trying to decide how to pay bills and not buy anything else, except groceries, until we could purchase without using credit. One of the first lessons I learned in marriage was that money causes many problems.

"Owe no man any thing, but to love one another . . ." (Romans 13:8). I pondered this scripture. *Does it really mean what it says?* It took several years for the Lord to teach me the truth of that verse.

There were arguments concerning how to spend, when to spend, how much to spend for groceries, about going into debt, and more importantly, how to get out of debt. Oh, the heartache and tears of being in "bondage" to money!

Buying groceries was a new experience each week. I knew how to bake and cook breakfast but little else. I learned how to cook rice and dried beans. Troy decided that I could cook rice and beans about as well as he had ever tasted. More importantly, we could afford rice and beans. We were paying bills first and buying groceries with whatever was left—which wasn't much, most weeks. (But ever so slowly, we were paying off the bills.)

Our first child, Glenn, was born two weeks early, and the insurance did not cover any of the doctors' fee or the hospital bill. The baby and I had problems from the start. He cried all the time and had very high fevers. I was breast-feeding, not realizing that my milk was bad. The doctor said he would have given me the necessary vitamins to produce healthy milk if he had known that I planned to breastfeed. He also told me how to mix formula for the baby and how to use a breast pump to dry up my breasts. (More unplanned expenditures.)

We had moved to a four-unit apartment building a couple of months before the baby was born. Our apartment was downstairs and had four large rooms. We bought a bedroom suite, a couch, and a chair on credit. We signed on the dotted line, and presto, credit and another bill! Satan said to us, "Everybody does it."

My parents gave us odds and ends to use in the kitchen. A nail keg with a homemade cover over it and a large apple box standing on its end was used for a chair. The families living in the other three apartments were not getting much sleep due to the baby crying all hours, and they began to complain to the landlord. Before long, we were asked to move. God had a plan (yet unknown to us) for our young family, and we began to look for a house. In answer to many prayers, we found a beautiful little house in a nice neighborhood close to the elementary school and stores. We looked at this house several times, but we did not have

a thousand dollars for the down payment. Dad reminded
me that there were several savings bonds (in my name) in
his safe deposit box at the bank. The bonds amounted to
about two hundred fifty dollars. We borrowed from the
credit union (where Troy worked) another two hundred
fifty dollars, and the company holding the mortgage on the
house told us that we could take out a second mortgage
for the balance of the down payment, which we did. The
regular monthly payment would be fifty dollars a month
for twelve years and another fifty dollars a month on the
second mortgage for one year.

We moved into our new home on Chestnut Drive when
Glenn was three months old. This was a residential neighborhood with many young families living there. Like us,
they had small children. Everyone had grass in the front
and back yards. Most of the neighbors had beautiful flowers
growing in their yards. Truly, the Lord had provided for
us, His children. In all these things, our tithe was always
given first.

Although we look and see hard times, God looks and
says, "Well done, good and faithful servant . . ." (Matthew
25:23). "Honor the Lord with thy substance, and with
the first fruits of all thine increase: So shall thy barns be
filled with plenty, and thy presses shall burst out with new
wine" (Proverbs 3:9–10). "Bring ye all the tithes into the
storehouse, that there may be meat in mine house, and
prove me now herewith, saith the Lord of hosts, if I will
not open you the windows of heaven, and pour you out a
blessing, that there shall not be room enough to receive it"
(Malachi 3:10).

Many people have said they can't "afford to tithe." My reply is, "I can't afford not to tithe," for I have learned that you can't out-give God.

We made friends in the neighborhood and attended Main Street Baptist Church. I began making curtains, and we were making do with what we had. We decided that we would purchase one nice piece of furniture each year. Our first purchase was a solid wood, maple dining table with six chairs. We paid cash and were so excited when it was delivered. We purchased the matching china cabinet the second year and were just as excited. We finally unpacked the wedding gifts of china and silver that had been so graciously given to us by friends and relatives. "Everything was so beautiful," I thought, and then Satan reared his ugly head.

Ever so innocently, the china cabinet and contents became more and more important to me and became my focus of admiration. It sat there like a shrine. I was convinced that if a fire started in our house, the china cabinet would be the first item to be saved. I was so proud that I could not see the danger. How could something so tangible replace my first love for the Lord Jesus? ("Pride goeth before destruction, and an haughty spirit before a fall" [Proverbs 16:18]. "Thou shalt have no other gods before me. Thou shalt not make unto thee any graven image. . . . Thou shalt not bow down thyself to (worship) them, nor serve them . . ." [Exodus 20:3–5].)

Years later, a sermon convicted me that there was secret sin buried deep within my heart, and it brought guilt and shame. On my knees, I sought the Lord, forsook my sin, and repented of the false pride. Forgiveness and renewal began to flood my soul, and I put my Savior back on the throne of my heart.

Glenn had his one-year check-up. He was a happy little boy, anxious to grow up. He had been walking for a couple of months and saying a few words. The doctor made a referral to an eye specialist for a routine exam. The eye exam revealed that Glenn had double vision in each eye. He saw two of everything (two mommies, two chairs, etc.). Strabismus, or cross-eyes, is a common defect in children. An imbalance in the action of the muscles that move the eyes causes one eye to turn in or out. Treatment for this condition sometimes requires surgery, exercises, and/or glasses.[6] Dr. Edwards explained surgery would correct the problem and that there was no danger involved.

We committed our baby to the Lord and made plans for him to have surgery at St. Luke's Hospital. Glenn and I played doctor and going to the hospital. We talked about the nurses, the hospital beds, the food served in your room, and new friends. He was ready for this adventure. He was a brave little boy when the time came for him to go to the hospital.

After surgery, Dr. Edwards told us that everything had gone well. He had cut the muscle in each eye and that Glenn would be sleeping the rest of the day. The next day he would be back in his room, would recognize us, and we should be there so that he would not be afraid. Dr. Edwards also said that there would not be any bandages on his eyes.

Troy went to the hospital before going to work the next morning. He heard loud crying as he was walking down the hall. He found Glenn crying, restrained to the bed, and his eyes bandaged. He became upset, untied Glenn's hands and feet, picked him up, and started rocking him. Glenn soon stopped crying. A nurse came into the room and demanded, "What are you doing? Put that child down."

Troy identified himself as Glenn's father and said, "Dr. Edwards told me that this baby would not have any bandages on his eyes this morning, and I refuse to stand here and listen to him cry after he has just had surgery."

The nurse said, "Everyone has bandages on their eyes after surgery, and he has to be restrained to keep him from pulling the bandages off."

I called the doctor to tell him what had happened at the hospital, and he assured me that he had taken the bandages off, the eyes looked well, and that he had written in the chart that bandages were not to be reapplied. He also said that he would call the head nurse on the floor and give her instructions again.

Glenn came home after a few days and we administered eye drops every four hours for a couple of weeks. Then he began eye exercises with a therapist at the doctor's office. He was fitted for glasses and told that he would have to wear the glasses until he started school. Dr. Edwards said that by then the eyes should be well and he would not need to wear glasses anymore.

Sure enough, before Glenn was six years old, his eyes were well, and he no longer needed the glasses.

Thank You, Father, for Your bountiful provisions.

*Chapter* 5

# PROTECTION

Whether we be afflicted, it is for your consolation and
salvation. . . . Whether we be comforted, it is for your
consolation and salvation.

—2 Corinthians 1:6

It was a hot Tuesday evening in August 1960. Troy had
worked all day and was then on overtime. Tuesday was
also payday. After the children (Glenn, three years old,
and Annette, sixteen months old) went to sleep, I took a
shower and went to bed also. I remember waking up lying
in a pool of ice and water. What woke me up? I began to
move my hands over the bed and pillows—everything was
wet. My mind was trying to process what had happened.
I couldn't remember, maybe I had set a glass of water on
the head of the bed before lying down and it turned over
and spilled all over me. Everything was dark and I couldn't
open my eyes. I got up and felt my way along the wall to

the kitchen, where the phone hung on the wall. I dialed Troy's work number. Troy answered the phone, and I said, "Troy?"

Troy dropped the phone, turned to his boss, and said, "Something is wrong at my house, I have to go home."

Troy's boss picked up the phone and began talking to me. I said to him, "I don't know what is wrong, but I can't see." I hung up the phone and felt my way back to the bed, and that was where Troy found me when he got home.

Troy had left work at once. His boss dialed "0" for Emergency and gave them our address. I heard a loud knock on the front door and Troy was calling my name, "Pat, Pat."

"I'm in the bedroom."

"Pat, open the door!"

"I can't—I can't see."

Troy had jumped out of the car, leaving the keys in the ignition. He ran back to the car, got the keys, and opened the front door. He began turning on lights as he ran into the bedroom. He saw me sitting on the bed, blood everywhere, my face and head twice the normal size, and he turned around and ran out the door.

"Help!" Troy cried. "Somebody, help!" he called over and over in a very loud voice.

In a few seconds he returned and sat beside me on the bed and softly began quoting the twenty-third Psalm. Several neighbors had heard him calling and came over to see what was wrong. Troy asked the neighbors to stay with the children (who were still asleep) while he took me to the hospital. It was well after midnight, but the neighbors agreed to stay until he returned.

He was leading me out to the car when an ambulance arrived. The paramedics put me on a stretcher in the back of the ambulance, and Troy sat beside me and continued to pray and quote the twenty-third Psalm.

The neighbors spent the remainder of the night washing the bedroom walls and ceiling (which were covered with spatters of blood), plus the trail of blood back and forth to the kitchen that I had made when I went to use the phone. They took all the linens off the bed and put them in the washing machine, threw the pillows away, and removed the mattress and box springs, which were soaked all the way through with blood.

Both the police and ambulance responded to the "0" for Emergency call. At the hospital, I did not comprehend what was happening. I was transported back and forth from St. Luke's Hospital emergency room to Duval County Medical Center emergency room and back to St. Luke's again. The county medical examiner was required to verify whether I had been raped or molested, and his office was at Duval County Medical Center. Thank the Lord, I had not been raped or molested sexually. Many doctors, nurses, and police were asking questions. Honestly, they all knew more than I did. I complained bitterly as they carefully cut my gown off and then did a complete examination. A plastic surgeon was called to do emergency surgery on my face and ear. Finally, near daylight I was admitted to a hospital room.

The headlines of the morning paper read, "Terror Reigns in Local Community. A young housewife was brutally beaten while her children slept in the next bedroom."

As the day progressed, I learned from the police what had happened. Someone, an intruder, had climbed through a dining room window. He heard noises as he began moving through the house and looked around for a weapon. He found a six-ounce Coke bottle sitting in the kitchen window. (The bottle was used as a hammer because it was so strong and not easily broken.) The intruder's intention was probably robbery, expecting cash from the paycheck. My pocketbook was found in the back yard, but a dollar and some change plus a small heart-shaped sterling charm were the only items missing. Our back yard was small, fenced, and had a gate that opened onto a railroad track. The track was a spur line, but the lumber mill used the track night and day to transport goods to and from the mill. The police thought that I must have dozed off to sleep, heard a noise in the house, and thinking that it was Troy coming home from work, roused and said something. The intruder possibly thought I would recognize him, so he used the Coke bottle as a weapon to beat me over the face and head. The beating continued until the bottle broke. My left ear was partially cut off, the left eye was cut, I had several cuts on my upper lip and face, and my nose was broken and cut badly. Each swing of the bottle threw blood across the ceiling and walls. The police said that the intruder left me for dead.

But a miracle had happened—the Lord had broken the bottle and spared my life. The broken bottle and the blood had seemed to me as ice and water on the bed. My face was a bloody mass, swollen twice the size, with no shape

PROTECTION

whatsoever, and when Troy saw me sitting there on the bed, he was terrified!

The police found a concrete block underneath the bathroom window from where, possibly, the intruder had watched me shower before going to bed. Tennis shoe tracks were found in the back yard, and the police thought the intruder might have walked the railroad track to the back of our yard and come in the gate. My purse was there also. After many months of investigating, no one was ever found or charged.

I was dismissed to go home from the hospital after about ten days. Troy asked, "Do you want to sell the house and move?"

"No," I said, "this is our home, and I want to go home."

Troy had burglar bars installed on all the windows and the glass inserts of the doors. God proved His love by providing deliverance from all fear. He had protected me from death during the attack, our children slept through the entire ordeal, and He delivered us from fear afterwards. How could I not trust Him? ("God hath not given us the spirit of fear; but of power, and of love, and of a sound mind" [2 Timothy 1:7]. "There is no fear in love; but perfect love casteth out fear: because fear hath torment. He that feareth is not made perfect in love. We love him, because he first loved us" [1 John 4:18–19].)

Troy and I frequently ministered at the City Rescue Mission in Jacksonville, and on our next trip to the mission, I shared how the Lord had saved me twice (once from sin at the age of thirteen and once from death at the hand of an intruder). After telling the above story, I sang "How Great Thou Art" by Stuart K. Hine.[7]

### How Great Thou Art
### Words and music by Stuart K. Hine

O Lord my God! When I in awesome wonder
Consider all the worlds Thy hands have made
I see the stars, I hear the rolling thunder,
Thy pow'r throughout the universe displayed,

> Refrain:
> Then sings my soul, my Savior God, to Thee;
> How great Thou art, How great Thou art!
> Then sings my soul, my Savior God, to Thee;
> How great Thou art, How great Thou art!

When through the woods and forest glades I wander
And hear the birds sing sweetly in the trees;
When I look down from lofty mountain grandeur,
And hear the brook, and feel the gentle breeze:

> And when I think that God, his Son not sparing,
> Sent him to die - I scarce can take it in:
> That on the Cross, my burden gladly bearing,
> He bled and died to take away my sin;

When Christ shall come with shout of acclamation
And take me home - what joy shall fill my heart!
Then I shall bow in humble adoration,
And there proclaim, my God How great Thou art!

For several months, Troy refused overtime work so he would be at home at night. I was sure that I would be fine but was grateful to have him home. But his first overtime night found me very nervous and anxious. My friend, Peggy, who had two children the same ages as Glenn and Annette and who lived a block away said, "I will stay with you tonight until Troy gets home." In fact, she refused to take no for an answer, and after her children were in bed asleep and her husband settled, she came to stay with me.

A few nights later, Troy had to work overtime again, but this time I took the children and spent the night at Peggy's house. What had happened to deliverance from fear? Was Satan trying to rob me of peace? I was convinced that I would not give in to his negative thoughts but trust God to complete that which He had begun in me ("Being confident of this very thing, that he which hath begun a good work in you will perform it until the day of Jesus Christ" [Philippians 1:6]. "Casting down imaginations, and every high thing that exalteth itself against the knowledge of God, and bringing into captivity every thought to the obedience of Christ" [2 Corinthians 10:5].)

After a few weeks, Troy said, "I have to work overtime tonight but will not be too late." The children and I stayed home that night, but I slept very little. I prayed for protection, for deliverance from fear, and that the Lord Jesus would remove all the negative thoughts that had filled my mind. Jesus was true to His word, and He confirmed in me the victory that He had originally given me. Peace, wonderful peace, filled my heart. ("But thanks be to God, which giveth us the victory through our Lord Jesus Christ"

[1 Corinthians 15:57].) Needless to say, we had no problem staying home by ourselves after that.

"Ye have not, because ye ask not" (James 4:2b). We limit the blessings that God already has waiting for us because we fail to ask. A fable, "Mr. Jones goes to Heaven," is told of a man who died and went to heaven. St. Peter was showing the man around—the mansions, the streets of gold—everything was so beautiful. The man noticed an odd-looking building with no windows and only one door. The building was an enormous warehouse. The man asked St. Peter to show him inside. St. Peter hesitated. "You really don't want to see what's in there," he told the new arrival. The man insisted that he be allowed to see inside. The door was opened, and they went inside. The building was filled with row after row of shelves, floor to ceiling, each stacked neatly with white boxes tied in red ribbons. Each box had a name on it. Of course, the man was anxious to find his name. He excitedly opened the box with his name on it and let out a deep sigh. There in the box were all the blessings that God had wanted to give to the man while he was on earth, but the man had never asked. (This fable has been paraphrased.)[8]

Lord, please bless and use me for Your honor and glory.

. . . . . . . . . . . . . . . . . . . . . . . . . . . . . . .

## Chapter 6

# TENDER MERCIES

It is of the Lord's mercies that we are not consumed, Because his compassions fail not. They are new every morning: Great is thy faithfulness.

—Lamentations 3:22–23

When our daughter, Annette, was born in 1959, she was diagnosed with a heart condition. How serious the problem, we did not know. We committed our beautiful little daughter to the Lord and His will, knowing that He wants only the best for us. She had two heart catheterizations before her first birthday. Her immune system was very weak, and every two or three months she was in the hospital with bronchitis or pneumonia. Finally, Dr. Roy Baker, a cardiologist, recommended that she be treated like a "hothouse plant," in order to avoid infection. "How do you treat a person, a baby, like a 'hothouse plant'? What does that mean?" I questioned the doctor.

Dr. Baker's reply was not encouraging, "She *must* be confined to the house."

"Impossible!" was my response. We were an active family with a two-year-old son in addition to Annette. But trial and error taught us. We could not take Annette anywhere around people, nor invite anyone to our house, with one exception. The grandparents, who lived out-of-town and visited occasionally, were encouraged to come as often as they could.

"We must keep Annette well long enough for her to go through surgery," said Dr. Baker.

Annette got a lot of rides in the car, which she loved, but she never got out of the car to go into a store or any place else, except the doctor's office.

Glenn and I went to church on Sunday mornings, and I taught a Sunday school class. Glenn and Troy went to church together on Sunday nights. Many times Troy and Annette rode for two hours on Sunday mornings until Sunday school and church services were over.

Annette did stay well and began to grow stronger, but she did not gain weight or develop normal childhood skills. My prayers and thoughts were that when she had surgery all these other things would follow. I spent a lot of time in prayer, not knowing what I should pray for, but asking that God's will be done in our lives.

Dr. Baker said to me on a routine visit, "Get a job and go to work."

"I can't do that," I replied. "How can we continue to treat Annette like a 'hothouse plant' if I go to work?"

"If you do not get a job, I will have you committed to Chattahoochee (a hospital in Florida for mental patients)."

We hired a full-time housekeeper and I began to look for a job. After several weeks, I went to work for the City of Jacksonville in the water department. It was an easy job but frustrating for me. I told Mama over the phone, "I do not like this job. The other employees act like children, always telling jokes and laughing."

She replied, "Pat, you have become a old woman, mentally. You have forgotten how to laugh and have fun. The years of confinement at home have made you old beyond your years. This job will teach you how to laugh again. Relax, do your work, and try to enjoy it."

For whatever the reasons, the housekeeper stayed about six weeks. To tell the truth I was glad she left. Troy soon found another housekeeper whose name was Thelma. Thelma was an attractive black woman with strong features, good with children, and also a good cook and housekeeper. She loved our children, soon became a part of our family, and stayed with us for about four years.

I had been working only a few months when Dr. Baker said, "It's time for Annette to have surgery." A team of heart surgeons began a series of exams and made plans for surgery. Annette's heart was very large and the major portion of blood circulated back and forth between the heart and lungs and did not flow throughout the body. The surgery would consist of cutting the paten-ductus, which should have closed after birth, but at least before one year. Annette's had never closed. (The baby's supply of oxygen from the mother is cut off following birth, and the baby must use his or her own lungs. The openings through the ductus arteriosus and foramen ovale are no longer needed, and they gradually close. In most infants, the ductus arteriosus closes within three months. The foramen ovale usually closes before the end of the first year.)[9]

Annette was a beautiful baby. Her face and head were the correct size for her age, but the rest of her body did not receive the life-giving blood needed to grow. The surgery would correct the blood flow to the entire body. Surgery was planned for April at Hope Haven Hospital. Annette would be four years old April 1963. How could I say no? I couldn't believe my ears. "Oh no! Please not Hope Haven, anywhere but there. I can not let Annette have surgery at Hope Haven Hospital." My response was so quick and emphatic that it took the doctor off guard.

"Hope Haven is one of the finest children's hospitals in the South and that is where we do all of our children's surgeries. What objections do you have?" asked the doctor.

"All my memories are bad," I explained. "Hope Haven is the hospital that treated children with polio, and I spent a lot of time there as a child. I just can't take Annette there."

The surgeon insisted that Troy and I go visit Hope Haven, see the changes, talk to the nurses, and then make our decision. "Hopefully, you will see a lot of changes. It is not the same as when you were a child," said the surgeon.

I didn't want to go look. My mind saw many sick, lonely children crying for their mothers who never came. Have there been times that you tell the Lord, "No, Lord, I don't want to do this, it is too hard for me"? I didn't want to pray about it. I didn't want to think about it. My mind was made up. After much soul searching, Troy finally convinced me to "just go look."

I could not believe what I saw. Was this Hope Haven Hospital the same place where I had spent so many weeks and months as a child? It was pretty and colorful. There were lots of pictures on the walls, toys, small tables and chairs, children running up and down the halls, and parents everywhere. The nurses seemed nice and helpful and answered questions and showed us around. We asked about visiting hours during and after surgery. The nurse said, "Parents are encouraged to spend as much time as possible with the child during surgery and recovery. We have learned over the years that children respond to their families and recover much faster when family members are present."

"Thank You, Lord, for Your patience with me and allowing me to see Your goodness at work," I prayed. Of course, we called the surgeon and said, "We are ready!" Annette had surgery and began to get well almost immediately. Blood began flowing throughout her body. She gained weight, learned how to help Thelma, and loved walking to the store and visiting neighbors. Annette's heart was getting well. Isn't God good. . . .

Our next trip to see Dr. Baker was exciting and scary. He was pleased with Annette's progress but wanted to do some testing. "Annette is too slow for her age," he said. "Haven't you noticed that she does not do things that other children her age can do?"

"Yes, I've noticed, but she will catch up. She is recovering quickly from the surgery," I said.

"No," replied Dr. Baker, "She is mentally retarded, you know. She will never totally recover. You may want to begin thinking about an institution."

I was speechless. What could I say? My heart cried, "No, never, never!" How do you pray, what do you say? Oh, Lord Jesus, what do we do now? ("Wait on the Lord, be of good courage, and he shall strengthen thine heart: wait, I say, on the Lord" [Psalm 27:14].)

Dad said, "We have no right to question why. Our family has not been singled out for this problem. Our president's family has a retarded sister, and we are not better than our president." ("If ye have respect to persons, ye commit sin, and are convinced of the law as transgressors. For whosoever shall keep the whole law, and yet offend in one point, he is guilty of all" [James 2:9–10].)

*Chapter 7*

# GRACE: BY DEFINITION, GOD'S UNMERITED OR UNDESERVED FAVOR

But the God of all grace, who hath called us unto his eternal glory by Christ Jesus, after that you have suffered a while, make you perfect, stablish, strengthen, settle you.

—1 Peter 5:10

Thelma stayed with us through two years of Annette's kindergarten and part of first grade. She loved our children. She read to them, taught them how to help with the chores: setting the table, dusting, and even scrubbing the hardwood floors. She walked with Annette to school every morning and home every afternoon. Annette was enjoying the little things that so often are taken for granted: having her own lunch box, being with other children, and going to school. She had a lot of catching up to do, and I was determined to make it happen.

The first grade teacher and the principal at North Shore Elementary School were nice, and I had high hopes everything was going to work out. Annette lasted about three weeks and then the principal called to say, "Annette has disrupted the class again and can not stay." There were few classes for special students, and children were placed at the principal's recommendation. There were long waiting lists for the special classes.

"Put Annette's name on the list," I said to the principal. "What can we do until her name comes up?"

The principal suggested home school. The teacher was helpful by providing books and lesson sheets. I quit my job and began home schooling for Annette. Annette's attention span was no more than five to six minutes; therefore, progress was slow. She wasn't happy to be doing school at home. She wanted to take her lunch box and go to "real" school with the other children.

We were looking for help—anything to promote growth in any area. Tap dancing classes for young children provided body coordination plus the opportunity to be with other children. Annette loved dancing class and did her best.

School proved to be frustrating. There were some good experiences and many bad ones. I learned that other parents had similar problems and also wanted the best for their children. Annette made friends through the years, participated in Special Olympics, and graduated from Alden Road Exceptional High School in June 1977.

She enrolled in Pine Castle, a training school and workplace for retarded adults. There were many different opportunities for learning trades: ceramics, horticulture, sewing, restaurant waiting and serving, hotel housekeeping, yard work, and contract services, such as Bank-America-Card mailings. Each trainee received a small monthly check. Annette worked at Pine Castle for a total of twelve years. She spent time in each training area and has fond memories of her days at Pine Castle.

During this time, Annette and I became members of the Jacksonville symphony. Once a month, we attended a wonderful musical program at the civic auditorium. We had good seats in the balcony, which provided a view of all that happened on stage. Annette looked very pretty all dressed up in her long gown and nice jewelry. This provided an opportunity for Annette to grow socially. The director of Pine Castle and his wife were also members of the symphony, and they complimented Annette continually on her many pretty gowns and how she was becoming a lovely young lady.

Annette rode the bus to and from Pine Castle. She and I had some special times together as we waited at the bus stop each morning. We memorized scripture or sang songs. One of our favorite verses was "He that dwelleth in the secret place of the most high shall abide under the shadow of the Almighty. I will say of the Lord, He is my refuge and my fortress: my God; in him will I trust . . . Thou shalt not be afraid for the terror by night; nor for the arrow that flieth by day. . . . For he shall give his angels charge over thee, to keep thee in all thy ways" (Psalms 91:1,2,5,11).

One Thursday afternoon, after Annette came home from Pine Castle, she called me at the office and asked, "Can I walk to the Pic N Save?"

The store was about four blocks from the house, and I agreed that she could go. "Call me again as soon as you get back home." I looked at my watch—it was 3:45 P.M., September 13, 1984. I arrived home about 5:20 P.M. Annette had not called, and she was not home.

Troy called the house from work and wanted to know where Annette was. He said, "I tried to call earlier and got no answer." I told him what I knew and that I was on my way to Pic N Save to look for her. Troy was working as a civil service security officer at Mayport Naval Station, which was located about twenty-five miles away. He worked shifts that changed every six weeks and was currently working the three-till-eleven shift.

I looked all over the Pic N Save and requested the management to page Annette over the speaker system, but Annette was not there. I walked the distance from the store to the house and asked each neighbor if they had seen Annette. Each one said that they had seen her going to the store but had not seen her return. I went back to the store, talked to the security guard, and asked if anything unusual had happened at the store that afternoon. I also talked to several store clerks. "Have you seen Annette this afternoon?"

"Yes, she was here earlier."

Where could she be? I called my friend and prayer partner, Eleanor Dinkins, and told her about Annette. "What else can I do?" I asked.

"Call the police and then call Troy," she said.

"OK, please start praying," I pleaded.

When we hung up, Eleanor called all the hospitals, and I called the police and then called Troy. I told the police what I knew, and they agreed to come to the house right away. The police questioned all our neighbors as to the last time they had seen Annette.

I began to pray that Jesus would be close, protect her, and keep her safe. I knew that she must be terrified wherever she was.

Eleanor called just as Troy was walking in the front door. She said, "Don't get excited, but there is someone fitting Annette's description in the emergency room at Duval Medical Center. She is listed as an unidentified person. It may not be Annette, but check it out."

Troy and I went immediately to Duval Medical Center emergency room (ER) and began asking about Annette. No one knew whom we were talking about. As we walked around in the ER, I saw something in one of the rooms that looked familiar—one bare foot. "Troy, come here," I said. "Look, that's Annette's foot."

"Are you sure?" he asked.

"Yes, get a doctor. I have to go in there." We finally found a nurse that was on duty when Annette was brought in and she took us in the room to see if in fact the person on the table was Annette. When we saw her, we knew at once that it was Annette. She was strapped to a large board and covered with a sheet. She had no clothes on, except for one sock. She did not recognize us. Her eyes were full of trepidation, she was incoherent, unable to talk and semi-conscious.

We were told conflicting stories about how she was found: 1) Some young men heard noises that sounded like a wounded animal in a wood thicket close to where they were fishing on the beach near Hecksher Drive. Upon checking to see, they discovered that it was not an animal but a person and called 911 to report what they had seen and heard. 2) A young man was riding a four-wheeler in the area and heard strange noises close by. He stopped to look, a young woman walked up, and together they began looking to see what the noises were. Upon investigating, they called 911 for an ambulance.

An ambulance responded and transported Annette to the county hospital as an "unidentified person."

## Chapter 8

# LONGSUFFERING

But thou, O Lord, art a God full of compassion, and gracious, longsuffering, and plenteous in mercy and truth.

—Psalm 86:15

We were told that Annette was on a trauma board, hands and feet restrained, and a stiff collar was strapped around her neck (all for her protection). The rape crisis center nurse and a GYN physician examined her and made x-rays of her entire body. The ER doctor said, "She would not have lived through the night if she had not been found when she was. She was in deep shock and the exposure would have been too great."

We sat for hours filling out papers, some for the hospital and others for the police. After all the paperwork was finished, I was able to stay by Annette's side. I held her hand and talked very softly, hoping that she could hear me.

Our friend, Becky Lindsay, and her daughter, Becky, came to the hospital and sat with us. They talked and prayed and gave us moral support as long as we were there. How thankful we are for Christian friends.

We were allowed to take Annette home sometime after 2:00 A.M. She soaked in a tub of warm water for half an hour and most of the dirt and trash came off her body. We then rubbed her down with mycitracin ointment to prevent infection. Annette still had not opened her mouth or spoken a word, and we didn't know what to do about the fear in her eyes.

The next day, when Annette woke up and went to the bathroom, Troy asked her if she knew who had done this terrible thing to her. She shook her head to indicate "yes." Troy asked several more questions and finally took her to the front door and asked her again who had done this. She tried pointing, and finally, in a weak, raspy voice said, "Shane."*

Troy called the police to let them know that Annette had identified the attacker. The investigator of the sex crimes unit with the Duval County sheriffs' office and some other officers came to the house to talk to Annette. Of course, they were unable to understand much of what she said. The police were in and out of the house for the next twelve hours, asking questions, using the phone, and writing reports. The hardest thing to deal with was the fact that no one believed Annette. They said to Troy and me that she was afraid to tell us that she had gotten into a car with a stranger because she did not want us to be angry with her.

At Troy's insistence, the police finally agreed to pick Shane up and give him a polygraph test, which he passed.

Shane was tall, blond, athletic, a handsome young man, and married to our next-door neighbor, Lily Mae.* He had no prior police record. Annette and Lily Mae were the same age and had been friends for more than twelve years. Lily Mae was pregnant and due to deliver any time. Poor Lily Mae, she couldn't understand why Annette would accuse Shane. He had always been nice to Annette in the past. *Lord, we all needed grace for this hard place* ("And ye shall seek me, and find me, when ye shall search for me with all your heart" [Jeremiah 29:13]).

I called the state attorney of the second judicial circuit and told him what had happened. He knew Annette well from the singles department at church. He wanted to talk to Annette, and as soon as she was able to talk, we took her to his office. He was convinced that Annette was telling the truth, and he had pictures taken of her body (for evidence). He assigned the assistant state attorney to the case because he thought it would be better for Annette to have a woman working with her.

I called Annette's physician to ask for medical advice. He suggested three scrubs a day in warm water with Betadine surgical soap and mycitracin ointment for the abrasions. Annette was looking much better after each scrub, except for her neck. Her neck was raw, and it was not healing.

A week later, my cousin, W. C. Blue, called and wanted to talk to Annette. W. C. worked for the department of agriculture as an investigator and was one of Annette's favorite cousins. He had heard from Buddy that the police did not believe Annette; therefore, he came to Jacksonville to see if he could help. He asked Annette to go for a ride with him. He also asked the investigator to go with them. As they rode, W. C. talked to the investigator and asked if she would mind if he talked to Annette and helped if he could. She said, "No, I don't mind, I have more of these cases than I can work, and I can not spend anymore time on this one. Shane has no record, he passed the polygraph, and there are no other suspects."

W. C. asked Annette to show him where she got into the car with Shane and to tell him what happened. Annette related the story from the very beginning: "On my way home from the Pic N Save, Shane stopped and offered me a ride. We were about two blocks from the house. He drove back to the Winn-Dixie to cash a check and told me to wait in the car. When he returned, he began driving in the wrong direction. He said he wanted to show me something. He drove out Hecksher Drive." Annette directed W. C. to make each turn from the store to the actual scene.

The investigator said, "We searched this entire area and found nothing."

W. C. started to turn into a thicket of trees, and Annette said, "No, not here, go further." Annette showed W. C. where to turn and said, "This is the place."

When they arrived at the place, the clothes she had been wearing that day (a light green pant suit with a shirt that buttoned down the front, a pair of white ankle socks, and blue slip-on canvas shoes), a purse, and a plastic bag from the Pic N Save with corn cheese and candy in it were found scattered on the ground. One shoe was up in a tree. There were signs of an incredible struggle. Suddenly, everything was different. The investigator now believed Annette. The next day Shane was picked up again, given another polygraph test using different questions, and this time he did not pass. He made a full confession and was put in jail. It was Thursday, one week after the abduction.

Lily Mae's father and stepmother brought her home from work that Thursday afternoon. I was watching for her to come home. *Lord, help. This is so hard for all of us.* I put my arm around Lily Mae and said, "I'm so sorry."

Lily Mae said, "Shane called me at work and told me he was in jail. I asked him if he had done it and he said yes. I also asked why and his response was that he would talk to me later."

Shane's mama was also at Lily Mae's house. She was crying and kept saying over and over, "Shane told me he didn't do it. He didn't do it."

Bail was set for $50,000 and a hearing date scheduled for October 1, 1984 at 9:00 A.M. The state attorney assured us that if Shane were able to make bail the judge would not allow him to go to his house or near our neighborhood. He also said that we did not need to be present at the October 1 hearing.

Annette was pleased to learn that Shane was in jail. All she said was, "Good, I hope he stays there!" We all got a good night's sleep for the first time in more than a week.

The neighbors had begun to gossip and make remarks. I was convinced that these remarks were a direct attack of Satan. He sure wanted to keep us upset and was doing a pretty good job of it. The rumor was that Shane would plead temporary insanity. The lady from the assistant state attorney's office called and talked to Troy. She said that she was assigned to represent Annette and wanted to talk to her. She also told Troy that the hearing for October 1 was cancelled, that the charge of kidnapping probably would not stick, and the charges of sexual battery were not going to be considered. Troy was angry and upset again. This whole ordeal had taken a toll on him. He was torn between taking the matter into his own hands and trusting scripture: "Dearly beloved, avenge not yourselves, but rather give place unto wrath: for it is written, Vengeance is mine; I will repay, saith the Lord" (Romans 12:19).

Annette had a doctor's appointment with Dr. MacLeod. He said that she had a second-degree burn around the neck (from attempted strangulation) and that she should have healed by now. The throat looked good inside; therefore, he recommended cold water soaks four times a day with a dolomite solution. He said that the hymen was in place and it did not look like a penetration was made, but there was an infection, so he wrote a prescription for Annette. All of this was good news but reinforced the fight and struggle that Annette had gone through.

The ladies from my Sunday school class and people from the church have ministered to us beyond our imagination. God is so good, and He just keeps showing us His love.

Becky picked Annette up to go to a Sunday school class party. They had a good time. It was Annette's first time to go out with her friends, and she had wondered how they would treat her. They loved her!

The assistant state attorney began working with Annette to get her ready for the trial. Annette did not understand many of the words that were used, but they were able to communicate.

Mama came to be with us the day after Annette came home from the hospital. She didn't say much, but listened to all our complaints, helped with the warm and cold water soaks, and kept meals on the table. I knew she was distressed, not knowing what else to do, and was not sleeping well. "I'm going home tomorrow," she said, "It has been a week and I'm more upset each day. I'll take Annette with me, if you think it would be OK. The change might be good for her, and we both need some peace and quiet." *Oh, Lord Jesus, help please!* I didn't want Mama to go. I was selfish; just knowing that she was near was a great comfort for me ("Then they cried unto the Lord in their trouble, and he delivered them out of their distresses" [Psalm 107:6]).

Annette and Mama returned from Perry after a week. Annette looked great—Mama looked so tired. The arthritis in her hip and foot were hurting, and she was having difficulty walking.

We all returned to work the week of October 8. Troy to his job at Mayport Naval Base, Annette to Pine Castle, and I returned to Duval County Health Department. Annette rode to and from the health department with me each day and caught the Pine Castle bus in the parking lot. Annette outwardly appeared to be handling everything OK.

The lawyers negotiated a plea bargain outside of court. Shane was sentenced to seven years. He was never to resume residence again on our street, Chestnut Drive, after release from prison.

Lily Mae had a beautiful baby boy, moved away, and filed for a divorce. Shane was paroled after three years, moved to another state, and married again.

Over the years, church friends have been our strength and our encouragers. As we read the Bible and grow in grace, we believe that God has given us a special gift—Annette is one of His angels. God also gave her a unique gift, the ability to "Rejoice with them that do rejoice, and weep with them that weep" (Romans 12:15).

We have never regretted our original decision to love, teach, and keep our daughter at home.

## Chapter 9

# ANSWERED PRAYER

And we know that all things work together for good to them that love God, to them who are the called according to his purpose.

—Romans 8:28

I was teaching a Sunday school class of ladies (ages fifty-five to sixty) who lived on the north side of town in Jacksonville. One of the ladies in our class was named Gertrude. She was a widow with seven boys. The youngest boy was in junior high school. She lived one block from the school and about two miles from the church. She walked or rode the city bus everywhere she went. As our class prayed for her salvation and ministered to her, it seemed that there were more and more reasons for her not to come to church. I began looking for excuses to go by her rental apartment just to say hello, and we soon became friends. I was praying, "Lord, show me how to minister to this precious lady."

As we became friends, she shared with me that five of her sons were in the state penitentiary and that she had lived a very hard life. I said, "Gertrude, the Lord Jesus loves you very much and can make your life brand new."

She replied, "You don't understand—you do not know anything about me. I have done too much."

Well, to tell the truth, I really did not know how to minister to Gertrude. I felt that she needed a better life more than anyone I had ever known, and certainly, God's Word promised that "if any man (woman) be in Christ, he is a new creature: old things are passed away; behold, all things are become new" (2 Corinthians 5:17). I continued to pray that the Lord would show me how to minister to Gertrude, and circumstances in my own life began teaching and leading me to the needed understanding.

My son, Glenn, was now twenty-eight years old, had been married for seven years, and he and his wife, June,* lived about eighteen miles from us. Everything was good in their lives, or so they told Troy and me. One day Glenn called me at work and said, "We want to come over Thursday night for supper. We have gotten into some trouble, but I don't want you to worry about it. I will tell you all about it when we come."

Why does a child ever tell a parent, *"I don't want you to worry"*? What else can you do? My heart had been very heavy for several weeks, and I had been praying, not knowing what to pray for ("The spirit also helpeth our infirmities; for we know not what we should pray for as we ought: but the Spirit itself maketh intercession for us with groanings which cannot be uttered" [Romans 8:26]). One night I could not get Glenn off my mind and could not sleep, so I spent most of the night in prayer asking God to take care of them and provide for their needs.

On Thursday, Glenn and June came over for supper. They looked like our children, even talked a little like our children, but told us nothing. Troy and I shared Jesus' love, our love, and our belief that the only way to be happy was by putting Jesus first in your life and home. Glenn said, "I have been thinking about that, but I do not want to make any changes in my life right now."

June hung her head and wouldn't make eye contact. Her only comment was, "I love Glenn, and we are not going to get a divorce." My thought was, *What does this mean?*

Finally, Glenn said, "We have been to court for some bad check charges and need to borrow some money to make the checks good. We've been put on probation, but everything will be all right."

We did not have the money to lend to them. We later learned that Glenn was sentenced to six months in jail and two and one-half years probation. June was sentenced to four weeks community service and one and one-half year's probation. Glenn was required to report to jail by 6:00 P.M. the following day. A week later, we learned that June's mother paid all the bad check charges in the amount of $1,800.

I had the most awful heartache. It wouldn't go away. The only tonic that helped was prayer. I could not keep a dry eye. I called Eleanor and said, "I need some strong prayer power."

Visiting hours at the jail were Sunday afternoons. Troy and I went to see Glenn. Troy did all the talking. I was not able to speak a word. Glenn told his daddy that he and June had gotten involved in dealing drugs. They did not have the money to pay and had started writing checks for cash to get the money. "We didn't know what to do," he said. "Getting caught was probably the only way out; we might have been killed otherwise."

Glenn requested the work-release program in order to keep his job. Each day he rode the city bus to and from the jail. He was allotted "x" number of hours to go and come from work. Troy and I continued to visit on Sunday afternoons. June was not able to visit due to community service on weekends. Glenn said that he pled guilty in order to plea bargain for June so that she would not have to serve time. During one of our visits, Glenn told us about washing some clothes the day before. He had no soap but he did get some of the dirt out. He slept on his clothes at night to keep them from being stolen. "Do you want me to wash your clothes for you?" I asked. The following Sunday, he had a plastic bag full of dirty clothes for me to take home, wash, and return the following Sunday. I cried as I put each piece in the washing machine. I washed them several times and they wouldn't come clean. I threw some of them away and some I patched. I was upset and angry. I prayed. I didn't understand why this had happened.

June filed for a divorce. The papers were served September 21, 1985, one month from the day that Glenn entered jail. Glenn was worried about June because she had missed some of her community service days. June's parents were trying to help her with the divorce and bills. Everything Glenn and June had was sold and a quitclaim deed was sent to Glenn to sign for the mortgage on their home and property. In spite of all that was happening, Glenn looked better than he had in a very long time. He was sitting perfectly still during our last visit, and his body had quit shaking.

Glenn registered to take a class entitled, "Learn to Read," two nights a week. There were men in jail who could not read and he promised to help them learn when he completed the class. As time went by, Glenn received permission to attend church on Sunday mornings. Later, he got permission for a day pass on Sundays. The jailer called our house to verify that Glenn was there and then asked to speak to him on the phone. Six months was an eternity for me, mentally. I thought my heart would break many times during that six-month period. ("There hath no temptation taken you but such as is common to man; but God is faithful, who will not suffer you to be tempted above that ye are able; but will with the temptation also make a way to escape, that ye may be able to bear it" [1 Corinthians 10:13].)

Glenn began putting his life back together before his release. At the end of the six months, he rented an apartment, got active in First Baptist Church, and began growing in the Lord. He studied his Bible consistently and was slowly making new friends. How thankful we are that we serve a God who gives us a second chance.

The still small voice of the Holy Spirit began to speak to my heart. It was time to visit Gertrude. "You now know how to share your heart with her heart," the Spirit said. During my next visit, Gertrude and I got on our knees in front of her couch, and she prayed to accept Christ as her personal Savior. The next Sunday, she walked the aisle and was baptized that same night. Praise the Lord! Our Sunday school class began praying for her sons in prison, and it wasn't long before Gertrude read a letter to the class telling of her sons' salvation. Gertrude got married again, her husband accepted Christ as Savior, and they began serving the Lord as a family. What a mighty God we serve.

The following letter was written June 7, 2001 and is printed here to illustrate the love and power of an Almighty God.

6–7–01

Ms. Pat Taylor,

My dear sister in Christ. Will drop you a few lines to let you know I haven't forgotten you. I include you in my prayers. I am still living on 9th Street. Hope you and all the family are doing great. I got your address from Eleanor. She comes by to see me now and then. I am so glad that she does. Praise Jesus for having friends in Christ. I am still walking and talking with Christ. All three children I have left are doing the same.

David, my husband, passed away the 19th of May. For a very long time I was taking care of him. I could not leave him by his-self [sic]. It was very hard, but thank God, he gave me strength to keep going. I just thank Jesus for all you ladies at Sunday school and for the teaching I got from you. I am just so thankful for all of you. My children are living in other states now. Just Jesus and me living alone. I would like to hear from you. Hope Troy and Annette and your son are doing fine. Hope you will come to visit me sometime. I just think of you every day and pray you are well and blessed each and every day and night.

Will stop my letter, but not my love.

Your sister in Jesus,
Gertrude

. . . . . . . . . . . . . . . . . . . . . . . . . . . . . . . . . .

## Chapter 10

# SONG OF JOY

Let the word of Christ dwell in you richly in all wisdom;
teaching and admonishing one another in psalms and
hymns and spiritual songs, singing with grace in your
hearts to the Lord.

—Colossians 3:16

The Lord has filled my heart with music! My earliest
musical memory was that of playing a small, gray,
plastic horn called a Tonette. Each child in the third
grade had an opportunity to participate in the Tonette band.
The only requirement was to purchase a lesson book and
a horn (Tonette). The Tonette band was the beginning of
many happy hours for me in the field of music. Soon after
that, I began piano lessons, then church choir, voice lessons,
and junior high and high school band. (I played oboe in
the concert band and snare drums in the marching band.) I
never had enough—I loved it! Dad and Mama encouraged
me and made all the lessons possible. Mama would say,

"Play the piano while I cook supper," or "Sing while we drive; it will make the miles go by faster."

Dad loved to hear the oboe with it's haunting sound. He would say to our guests, "Pat can play the oboe for us." It was a production to get the horn out, put it together, soak the reed, find some music, and then begin to blow. The attention was exciting, but many times all that came out was squeaks.

Music has always been a very important part of worship for me and is also a calming relief from stress. The hymns of faith were a schoolmaster teaching me to depend upon God. During my working years, I would come home for lunch and sit at the piano and play for half an hour from the church hymnal and be totally refreshed. ("David took a harp, and played with his hand: so Saul was refreshed, and was well, and the evil spirit departed from him" [1 Samuel 16:23b].)

I sang for weddings, funerals, worship services, young people's meetings, camp meetings, and every other time there was an opportunity. We sang as a family for personal enjoyment and also for other activities. When friends visited, we always gathered around the piano and sang, sometimes for hours.

Once I was asked to sing for a funeral of a twelve-year-old boy who had died with muscular dystrophy. He had heard "A Crippled Boy's Prayer" by William L. Carter over the radio and told his mother that he wanted to go to heaven to be like all the other children (strong and healthy). I had never heard that song but purchased a copy of the music, and Glenn and I sang it at his funeral. The words were beautiful and had a message for me: 1) my feet and legs will both be the same in heaven, and 2) Annette will be completely whole. We will be like Jesus.

God's promise of heaven is for everyone who believes that Jesus is the Son of God and accepts Him as his or her Saviour.

God gave me songs to sing through all of life's experiences. There were many valleys to walk through that have not been mentioned in this book, and the Lord Jesus has been faithful through them all. There were equally as many mountaintop experiences that were enjoyed to the fullest. I thank God for each mountaintop, but the valleys have kept me on my knees. The Lord Jesus has been teaching me how to be like Him, and He never makes a mistake. ("Wherein ye greatly rejoice, though now for a season, if need be, ye are in heaviness through manifold temptations: That the trial of your faith, being much more precious than of gold that perisheth, though it be tried with fire, might be found unto praise and honour and glory at the appearing of Jesus Christ" [1 Peter 1:6–7].)

Thank You, Father, for counting me worthy to suffer, to grow, and to learn: "They were counted worthy to suffer shame for his name" (Acts 5:41b).

Songs of testimony became my soul's cry to our heavenly Father and also a sharing of my heart for others. When I sang in public, I wanted the Lord Jesus to be pleased, and many times the Holy Spirit would express Himself through tears of love and praise as I sang. A few of my favorites were: "Each Step I Take" by W. Elmo Mercer, "I Have Found A Hiding Place" by Gladys Blanchard Muller, "Why Should He Love Me So?" by Robert Harkness, "He Just Loved Me

More And More" by Colbert and Joyce Croft, "Now I Belong to Jesus" by Norman J. Clayton, "Have You Had A Gethsemane?" by William J. Gaither, and "Fill My Cup Lord" by Richard Blanchard.

"Tears Are a Language (God Understands)" by Gordon Jensen helped me through times of personal trouble and sorrow. Just knowing that God understands and wants me to draw close to Him in prayer (tears and all) eases the hurt and allows me to wait for His answers.

"Humble Thyself to Walk With God" by Johnson Oatman, Jr., and W. J. Rogers taught me not to think of myself more highly than I ought to think but to depend upon the Lord Jesus more and more, day by day.

Jesus must be Lord of all or He is not Lord at all.

### Humble Thyself to Walk with God
### Words by Johnson Oatman, Jr.,
### Music by W. J. Rogers

If thou wouldst have the dear Savior from heaven
Walk by thy side from the morn till the even,
There is a rule that each day you must follow:
Humble thyself to walk with God.

> Refrain
> Humble thyself and the Lord will draw near thee,
> Humble thyself and his presence shall cheer thee:
> He will not walk with the proud or the scornful,
> Humble thyself to walk with God.

Just as the Lord in the world's early ages
Walked and communed with the prophets and sages,

He will come now if you meet the conditions:
Humble thyself to walk with God.

> Just as the stream finds a bed that is lowly,
> So Jesus walks with the pure and the holy;
> Cast out thy pride, and in heartfelt contrition
> Humble thyself to walk with God. [10]

Humility is a hard lesson and not easily learned. "For I say, through the grace given unto me, to every man that is among you, not to think of himself more highly than he ought to think; but to think soberly, according as God hath dealt to every man the measure of faith" (Romans 12:3). "For if a man think himself to be something, when he is nothing he deceiveth himself" (Galatians 6:3).

During the time Annette was treated as a "hot house" plant, we attended a small church with less than a hundred members. We could sit in the back of the church and take Annette out as soon as the service was over. We were enjoying the fellowship and the people expressed a sincere love for God and His Son.

I began praying about a place of service. After church one Sunday, I spoke to the pastor regarding some area of service that I could fulfill. He replied, "What would you like to do?"

I was totally surprised by the words that came out of my mouth. "I would like to organize a junior choir; practice one afternoon a week and let them sing on Sunday nights."

The pastor was enthusiastic, "That will be great. Decide how you will get the children to the church for practice and home afterwards and then we will make an announcement to the parents."

The idea of a junior choir had never entered my mind and when it came out of my mouth, I was shocked. ("…take ye no thought how or what thing ye shall answer, or what ye shall say: For the Holy Ghost shall teach you in the same hour what ye ought to say." [Luke 12:11b-12].)

We accomplished the task with God's leading, and the boys and girls loved having their own choir, choir robes, and singing in church on Sunday nights. The parents were appreciative and encouraging. (They picked the children up from the church after practice each week and were always available when asked to bring refreshments.)

"Born to Serve the Lord" by Bud Chambers has become a testimony of my life and identifies me as a child of the King. Satan knows that I was bought with a price, the precious blood of Jesus on the cross of Calvary—but he never gives up. He wants to destroy my testimony and take away my joy; therefore, there is the need for daily prayer and Bible study, without which there is no spiritual growth and no joy.

Later years have introduced me to a new type of music; that of playing hand bells. The tone is rich and melodious, and it takes many people (each person playing one or two bells each) to create beautiful music. As much as I personally enjoy music, I acknowledge that it is one of God's gifts and I must be faithful and responsible in my service to Him through music. Blessings are only received as God the Holy Spirit puts the music in my heart and mouth and is allowed to minister to whom He will. "Whatsoever thy hand findeth to do, do it with thy might . . ." (Ecclesiastes 9:10a).

# REFERENCES

## Chapter 2

1. State of Florida, Office of Vital Statistics, 1940.
2. *The World Book Encyclopedia*, s.v., 1969, Polio-myelitis.
3. *The World Book Encyclopedia*, s.v., 1969, Polio-myelitis.
4. U.S. Department of Health & Human Services, July 2000.
5. Immunization Schedule published annually by Centers for Disease Control.

## Chapter 4

6. *The World Book Encyclopedia*, s.v., 1969, Defects and Diseases of the Eye.

## Chapter 6

8. Bruce Wilkinson, *The Prayer of Jabez*, (Sisters, OR: Multnomah Publishers, Inc., 2000), 25–27.
9. *The World Book Encyclopedia*, s.v., 1969, Development of the Heart.

## Chapter 10

10. Johnson Oatman, Jr., and J. W. Rogers, HYMNAL *of the Church of God*, (Anderson IN., Warner Press, Inc., 1909, 1953).

## Permissions
## Chapter 5

7. S. K. Hine, "How Great Thou Art." Assigned to Manna Music, Inc., 35255 Brooten Road, Pacific City, OR 97135. Copyright 1953. Renewed 1981 by Manna Music, Inc. All Rights Reserved. Used by Permission. (ASCAP)

To order additional copies of

Have your credit card ready and call

Toll free: (877) 421-READ (7323)

or order online at: www.winepressbooks.com

A percentage of book sales will be donated to
Children's Home Ministries.